W9-CPM-841

GRAPHIC HISTORY

DOLLEY MADISON
SAVES HISTORY

by Roger Smalley

illustrated by Anna Maria Cool,
Scott Rosema, and Charles Barnett III

Consultant: Kenneth Madison Clark, Historical Consultant,
The James Madison Museum
Orange, Virginia

Capstone
press
Mankato, Minnesota

Graphic L… ne Press,
151 Good Counsel … , Minnesota 56002.

Printed in the United States of America

1 2 3 4 5 6 10 09 08 07 06 05

Library of Congress Cataloging-in-Publication Data
Smalley, Roger.
Dolley Madison saves history / by Roger Smalley; illustrated by Anna Maria Cool, Scott Rosema, Charles Barnett III.
p. cm. —(Graphic library. Graphic history)
Includes bibliographical references and index.
ISBN 0-7368-4972-6 (hardcover)
1. Madison, Dolley, 1768–1849—Juvenile literature. 2. Presidents' spouses—United States—Biography—Juvenile literature. 3. United States—History—War of 1812—Juvenile literature. 4. Washington (D.C.)—History—Capture by the British, 1814—Juvenile literature. I. Cool, Anna Maria. II. Rosema, Scott. III. Barnett, Charles, III. IV. Title. V. Series.
E342.1.S63 2006
973.5'1'092—dc22 2005008465

Summary: The story of Dolley Madison's actions during the War of 1812 is told in a graphic novel format.

Art and Editorial Direction
Jason Knudson and Blake A. Hoena

Designers
Bob Lentz and Juliette Peters

Colorist
Sarah Trover

Editor
Sarah L. Schuette

Editor's note: Direct quotations from primary sources are indicated by a yellow background.

Direct quotations appear on the following pages:
Pages 4, 8, 11, 17, 19, 25 from *The Selected Letters of Dolley Payne Madison* by Dolley Madison (Charlottesville, VA: University of Virginia Press, 2003.).
Pages 6, 9, 13 from *The First Forty Years of Washington Society in the Family Letters of Margaret Bayard Smith* by Margaret Bayard Smith (New York: F. Ungar, 1965).
Pages 21, 23 from *The Burning of Washington: The British Invasion of 1814* by Anthony S. Pitch (Annapolis, MD: Naval Institute Press, 1998).

TABLE OF CONTENTS

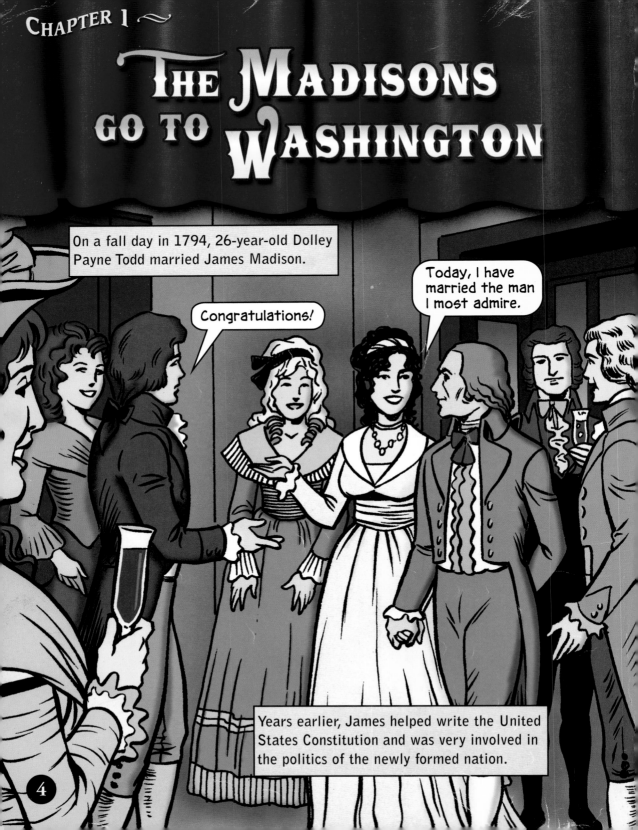

Chapter 1

The Madisons Go to Washington

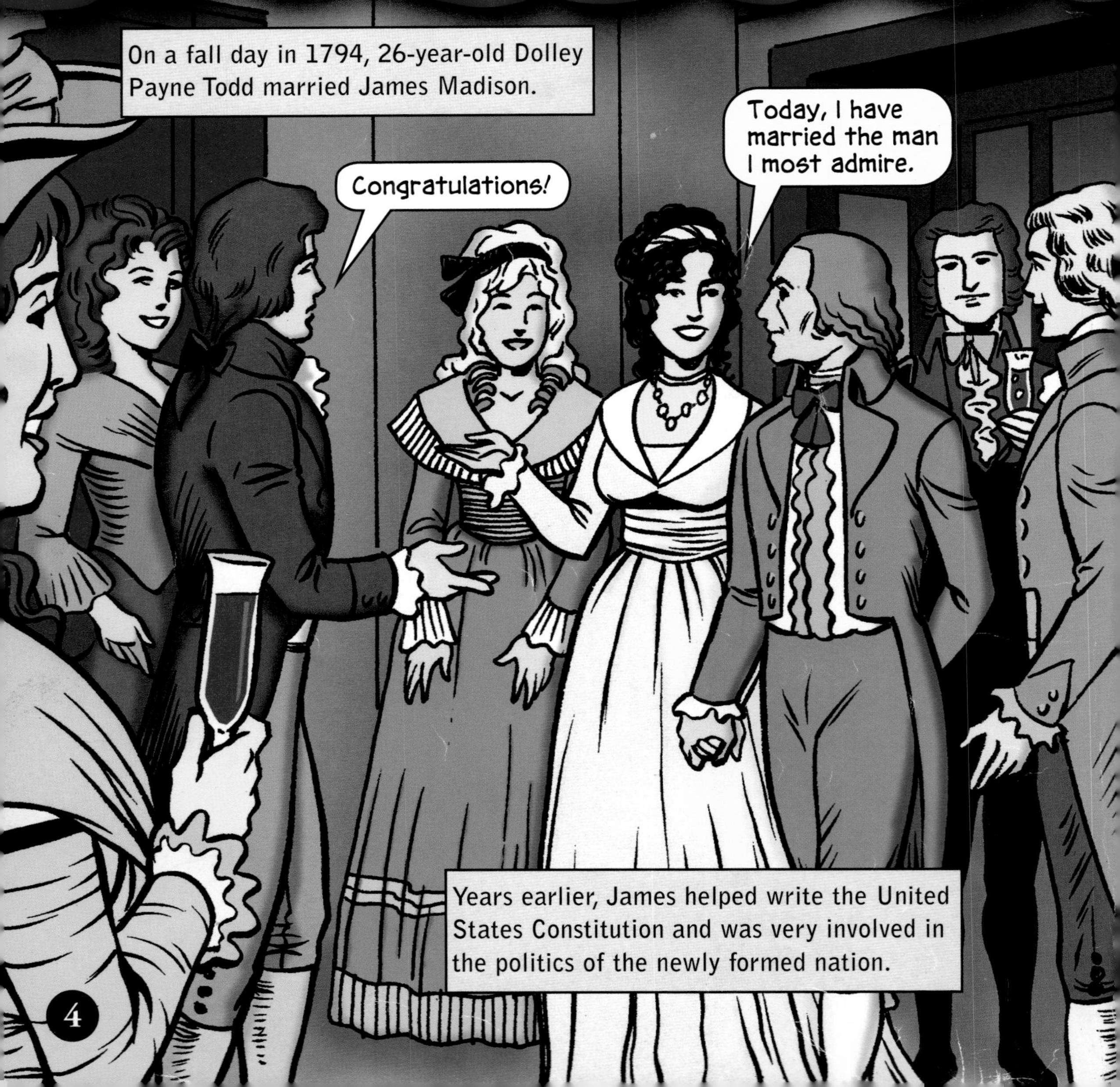
On a fall day in 1794, 26-year-old Dolley Payne Todd married James Madison.
Congratulations!
Today, I have married the man I most admire.
Years earlier, James helped write the United States Constitution and was very involved in the politics of the newly formed nation.

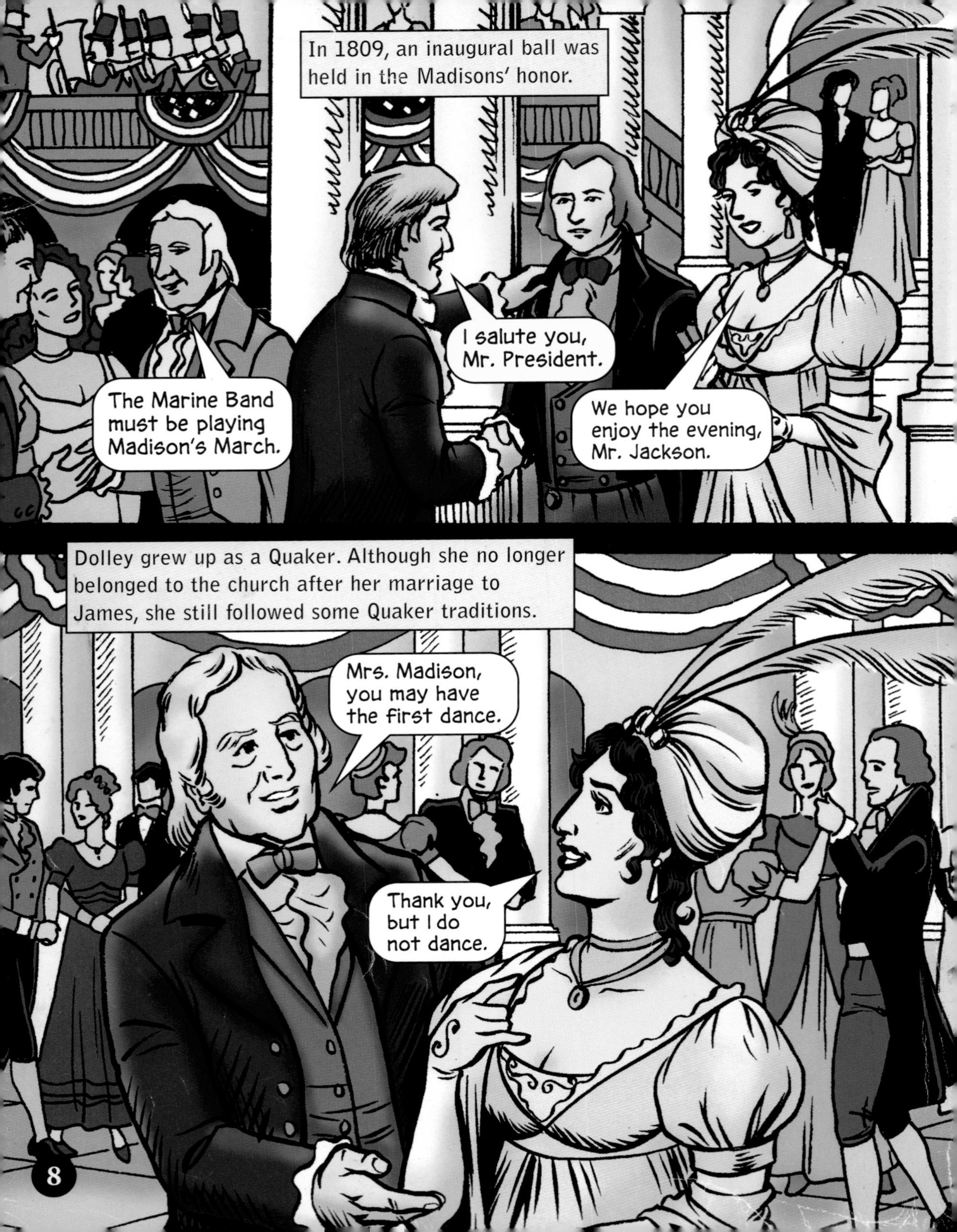
In 1809, an inaugural ball was held in the Madisons' honor.
The Marine Band must be playing Madison's March.
I salute you, Mr. President.
We hope you enjoy the evening, Mr. Jackson.
Dolley grew up as a Quaker. Although she no longer belonged to the church after her marriage to James, she still followed some Quaker traditions.
Mrs. Madison, you may have the first dance.
Thank you, but I do not dance.

Chapter 3

Danger in Washington, D.C.

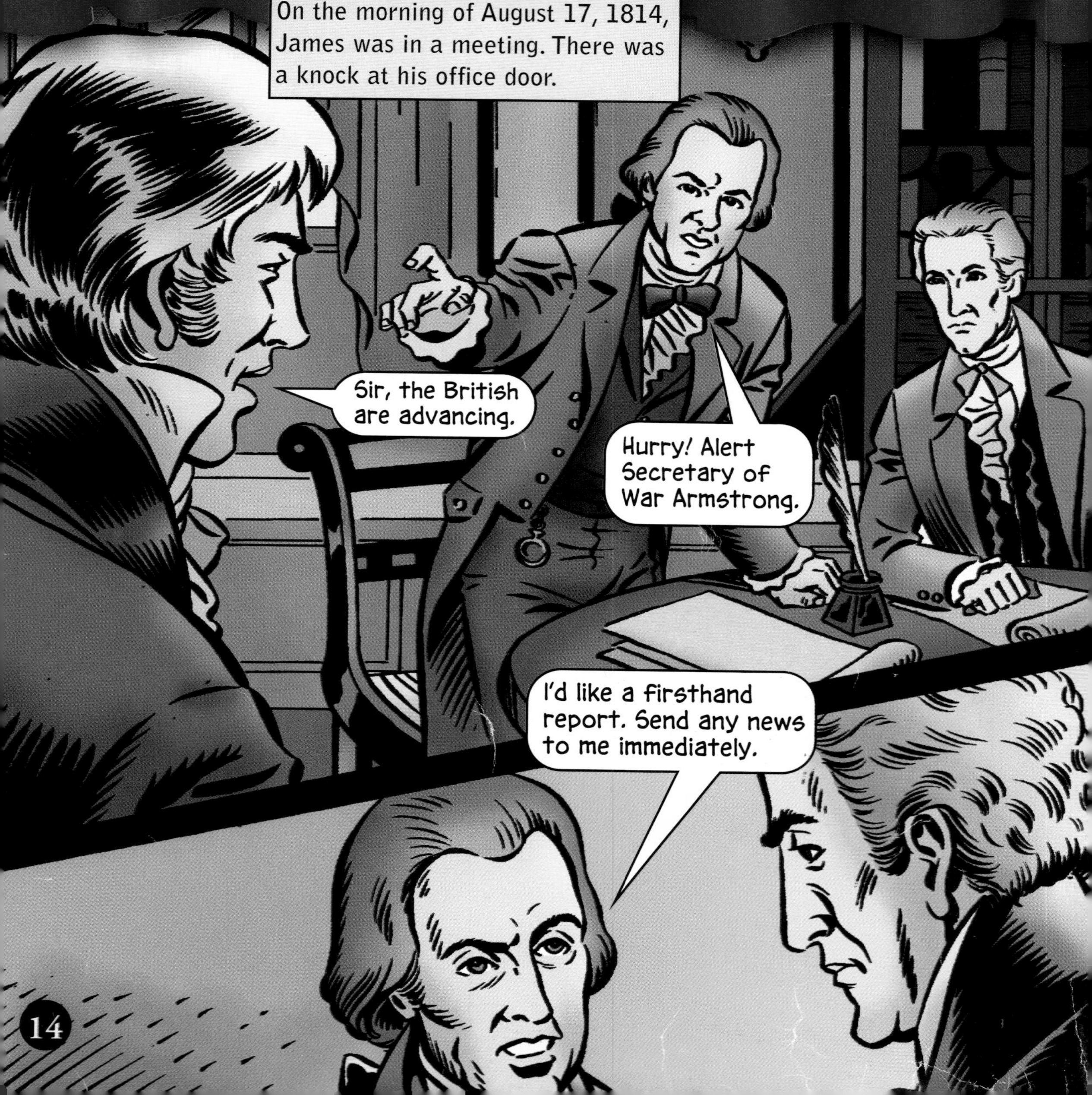
On the morning of August 17, 1814, James was in a meeting. There was a knock at his office door.
Sir, the British are advancing.
Hurry! Alert Secretary of War Armstrong.
I'd like a firsthand report. Send any news to me immediately.

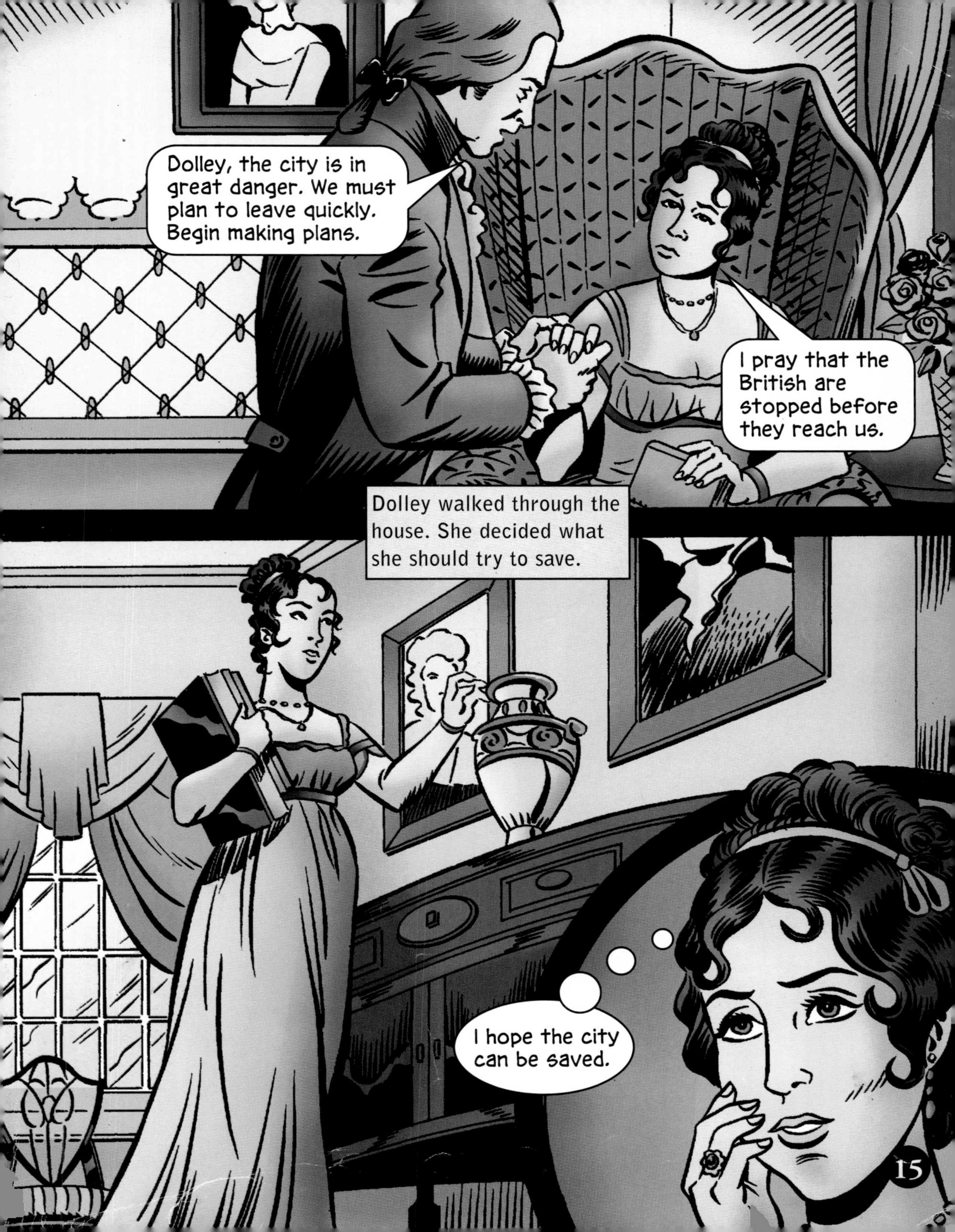
Dolley, the city is in great danger. We must plan to leave quickly. Begin making plans.
I pray that the British are stopped before they reach us.
Dolley walked through the house. She decided what she should try to save.
I hope the city can be saved.

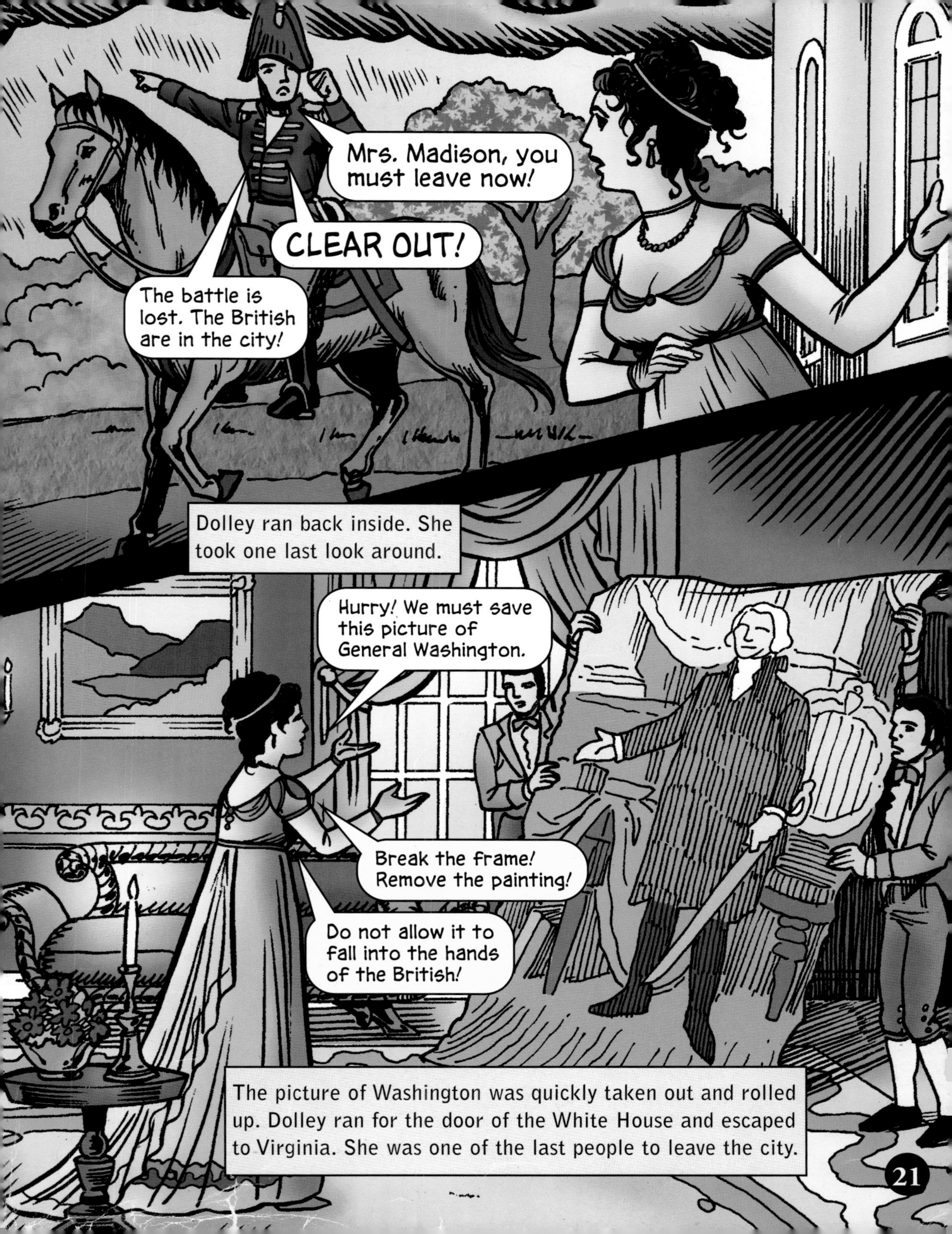
Mrs. Madison, you must leave now!
CLEAR OUT!
The battle is lost. The British are in the city!
Dolley ran back inside. She took one last look around.
Hurry! We must save this picture of General Washington.
Break the frame! Remove the painting!
Do not allow it to fall into the hands of the British!
The picture of Washington was quickly taken out and rolled up. Dolley ran for the door of the White House and escaped to Virginia. She was one of the last people to leave the city.

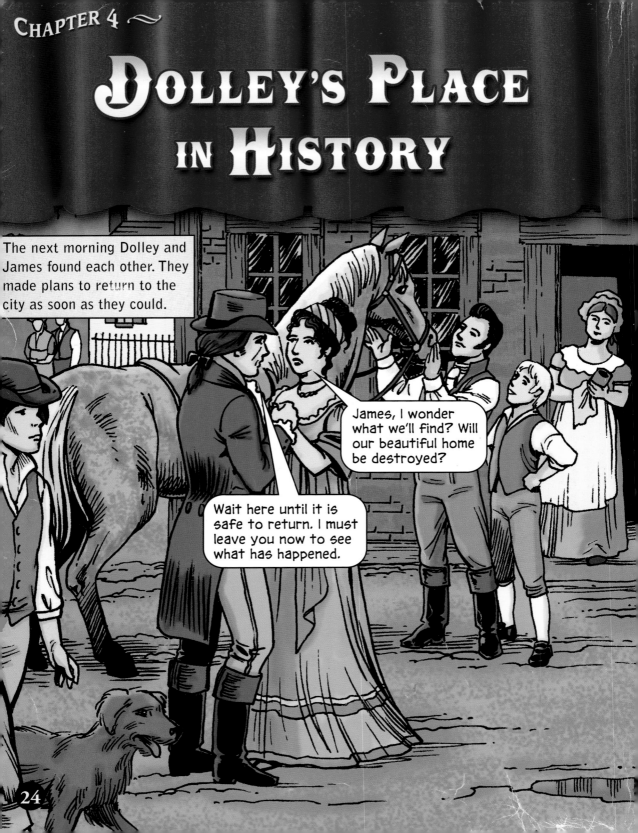

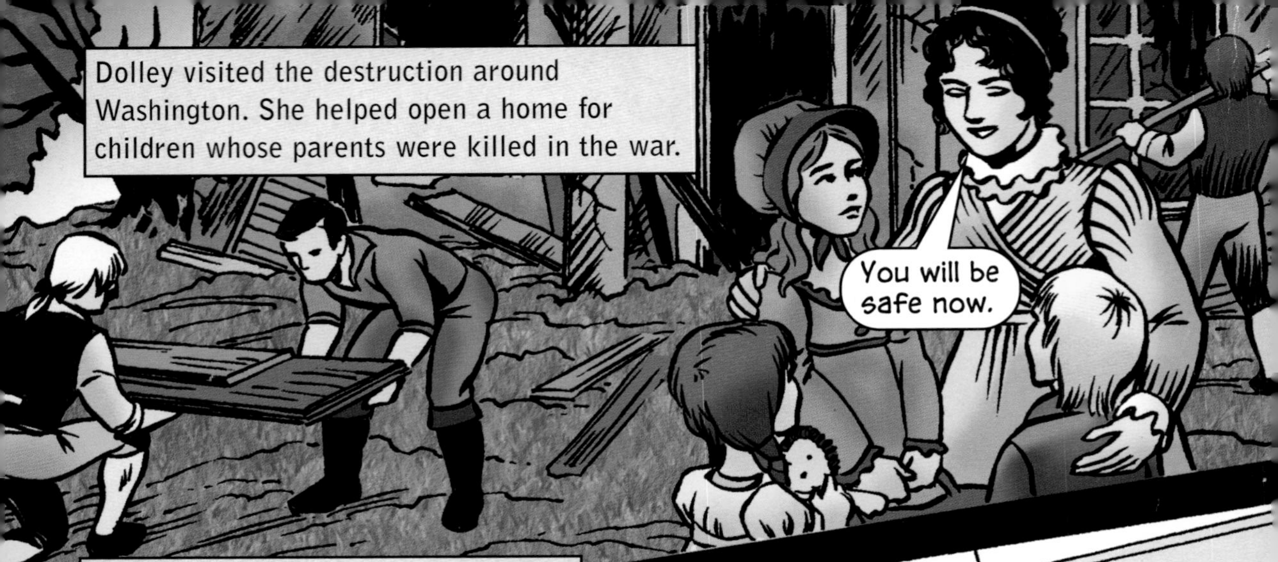
Dolley visited the destruction around Washington. She helped open a home for children whose parents were killed in the war.
You will be safe now.

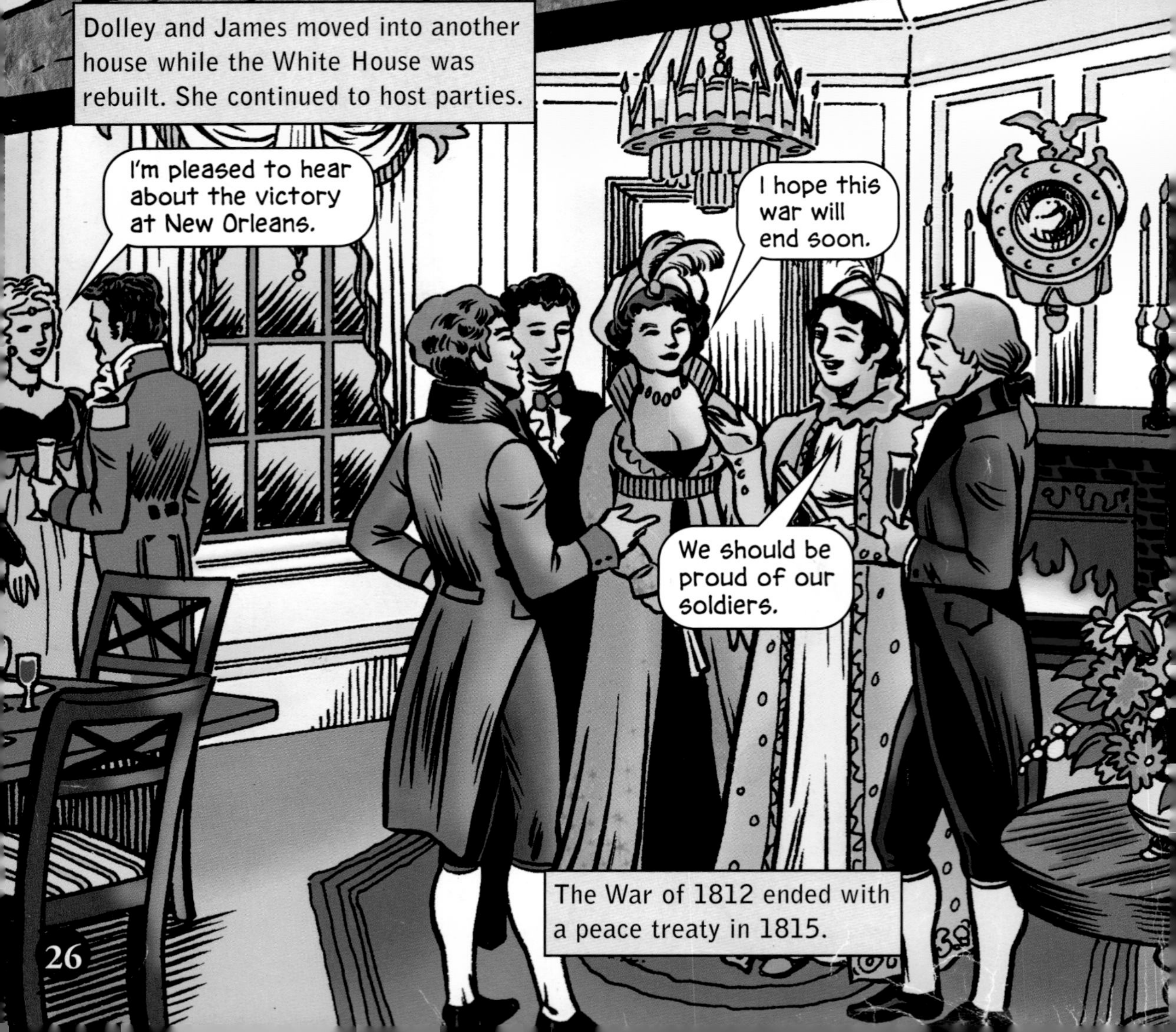
Dolley and James moved into another house while the White House was rebuilt. She continued to host parties.
I'm pleased to hear about the victory at New Orleans.
I hope this war will end soon.
We should be proud of our soldiers.
The War of 1812 ended with a peace treaty in 1815.

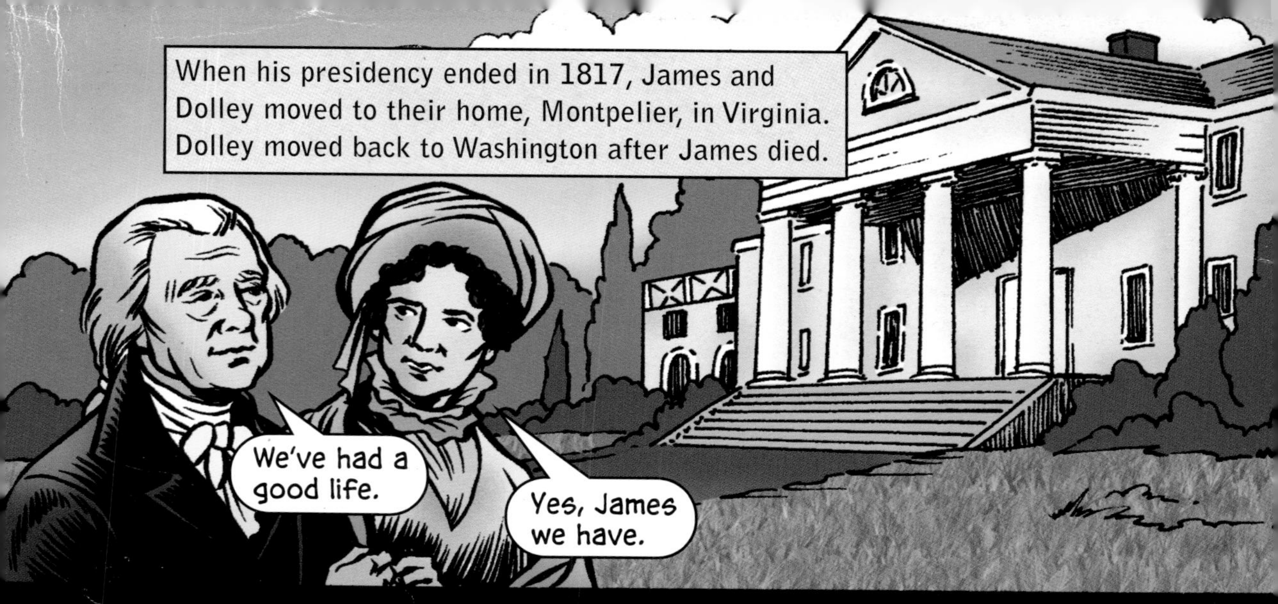
When his presidency ended in 1817, James and Dolley moved to their home, Montpelier, in Virginia. Dolley moved back to Washington after James died.
We've had a good life.
Yes, James we have.

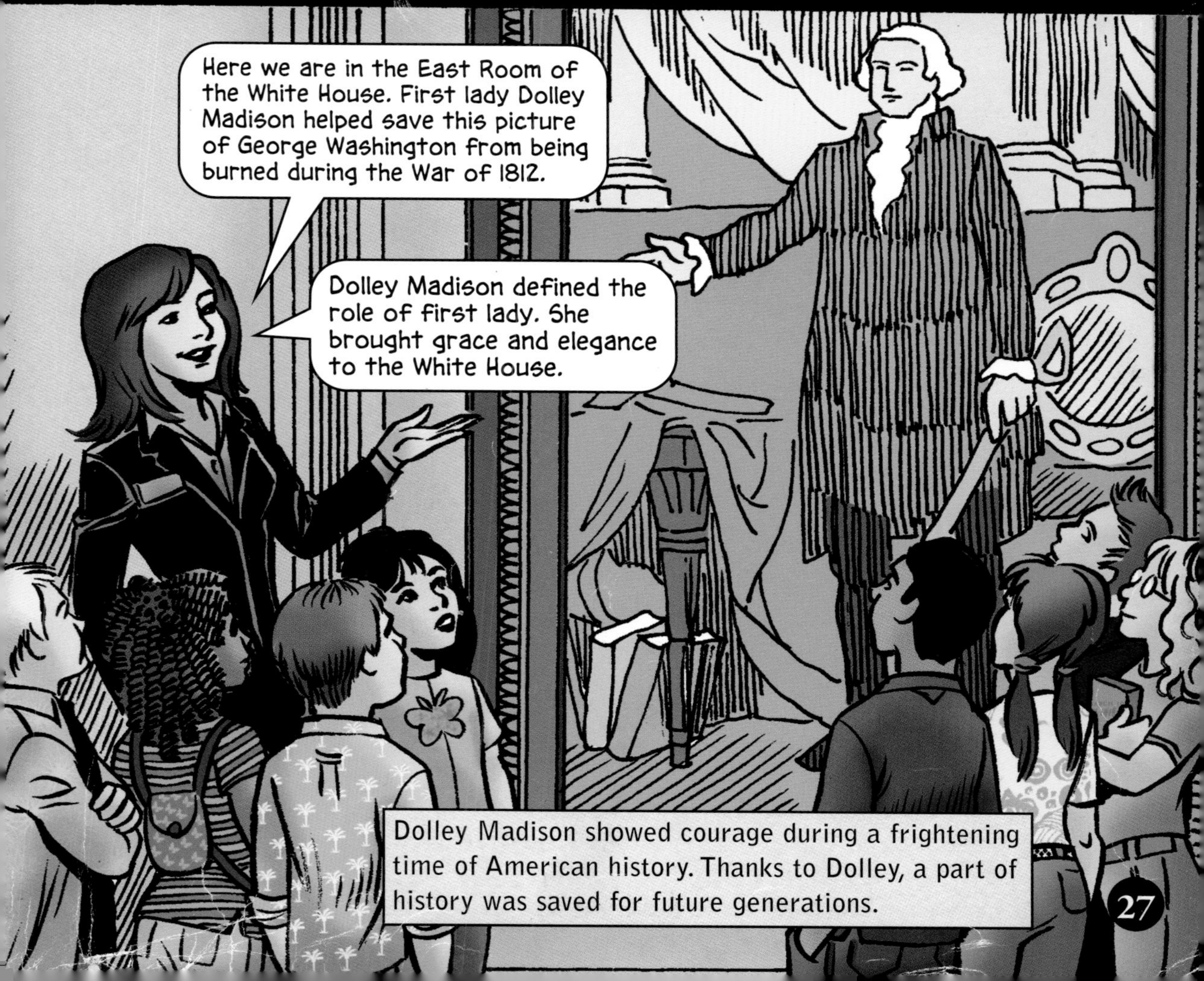
Here we are in the East Room of the White House. First lady Dolley Madison helped save this picture of George Washington from being burned during the War of 1812.
Dolley Madison defined the role of first lady. She brought grace and elegance to the White House.
Dolley Madison showed courage during a frightening time of American history. Thanks to Dolley, a part of history was saved for future generations.

More about ~ DOLLEY MADISON

~ Dolley was born on May 20, 1768, in North Carolina. She died on July 12, 1849. She is buried next to James at Montpelier. Today, Montpelier serves as a National Historic Site.

~ Dolley's first husband, John Todd, and son William Temple died of yellow fever. Payne Todd, Dolley's oldest son, survived.

~ Dolley hosted the first presidential inaugural ball in 1809. Tickets cost $4. More than 400 guests were invited. The Marine Band, America's oldest professional organization, played for the event. It has played for every inaugural ball since.

~ Dolley served American foods at her parties. Meals including smoked Virginia ham, baked sweet corn, Boston baked beans, and New England maple syrup were prepared. Ice cream and cake were popular desserts of the time.

- The only personal item Dolley saved from the White House before it burned was a small clock. All of her clothing and other personal belongings were left and burned.

- After the burning of the White House, James considered moving the capital back to Philadelphia. Dolley encouraged him to keep it in Washington, D.C.

- Later in her life, Dolley was given many honors for her service to the United States. On January 8, 1844, the House of Representatives gave Dolley an honorary seat in the House Chamber at the Capitol. At the time, it was the highest honor ever given to an American woman.

- Dolley was given another honor when a new invention, the telegraph, was demonstrated for the first time. She sent the first private message by telegraph.

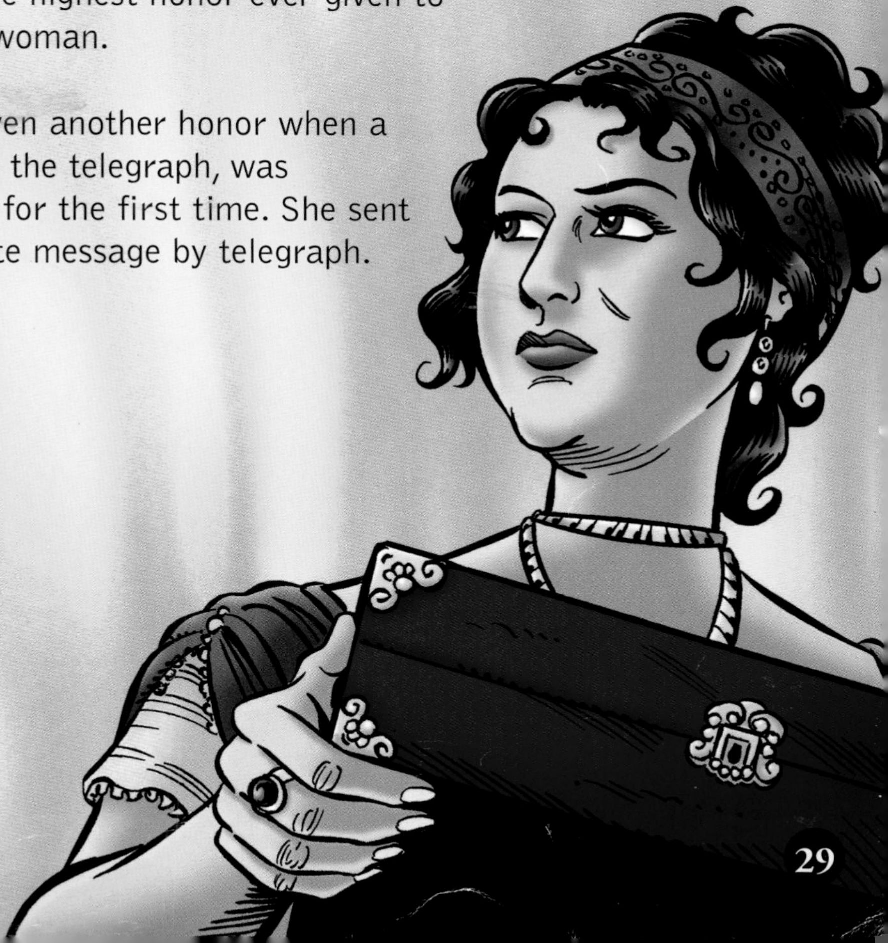

GLOSSARY

capital (KAP-uh-tuhl)—a city where the government of a country is based; Philadelphia was the capital of the United States before it was moved to Washington, D.C.

Congress (KONG-griss)—the branch of government that makes laws

fleet (FLEET)—a group of warships

hostess (HOH-stuhss)—a woman who entertains guests at parties or other social events

Quaker (KWAY-kur)—a member of the religious group also called the Society of Friends; Quakers follow simple religious services and oppose war.

INTERNET SITES

FactHound offers a safe, fun way to find Internet sites related to this book. All of the sites on FactHound have been researched by our staff.

Here's how:

1. *Visit www.facthound.com*
2. Type in this special code **0736849726** for age-appropriate sites. Or enter a search word related to this book for a more general search.
3. Click on the **Fetch It** button.

FactHound will fetch the best sites for you!

READ MORE

Ashby, Ruth. *James and Dolley Madison.* Presidents and First Ladies. Milwaukee: World Almanac Library, 2005.

Modifica, Lisa. *A Timeline of the White House.* Timelines of American History. New York: Rosen, 2004.

Raatma, Lucia. *The War of 1812.* We the People. Minneapolis: Compass Point Books, 2005.

BIBLIOGRAPHY

Arnett, Ethel Stephens. *Mrs. James Madison: The Incomparable Dolley.* Greensboro, NC: Piedmont Press, 1972.

Gerson, Noel B. *The Velvet Glove: A Life of Dolley Madison.* Nashville: Thomas Nelson, 1975.

Madison, Dolley. *The Selected Letters of Dolley Payne Madison.* Charlottesville, VA: University of Virginia Press, 2003.

Pitch, Anthony S. *The Burning of Washington: The British Invasion of 1814.* Annapolis, MD: Naval Institute Press, 1998.

Smith, Margaret Bayard. *The First Forty Years of Washington Society in the Family Letters of Margaret Bayard Smith.* New York: F. Ungar, 1965.

Index